My First Animal Library

Toucans

by Mari Schuh

Bullfrog
Books

Ideas for Parents and Teachers

Bullfrog Books let children practice reading informational text at the earliest reading levels. Repetition, familiar words, and photo labels support early readers.

Before Reading

- Discuss the cover photo. What does it tell them?
- Look at the picture glossary together. Read and discuss the words.

Read the Book

- "Walk" through the book and look at the photos. Let the child ask questions. Point out the photo labels.
- Read the book to the child, or have him or her read independently.

After Reading

- Prompt the child to think more. Ask: Have you ever seen a toucan? Do you know other birds with big beaks?

Dedicated to St. Lucy Parish School. —MS

Bullfrog Books are published by Jump!
5357 Penn Avenue South
Minneapolis, MN 55419
www.jumplibrary.com

Library of Congress Cataloging-in-Publication Data
Schuh, Mari C., 1975- author.
  Toucans / by Mari Schuh.
    pages cm.—(My first animal library)
  Summary: "This photo-illustrated book for early readers describes how a toucan's big, bright bill helps it survive in the rain forest"—Provided by publisher.
  Audience: Ages 5-8.
  Audience: K to grade 3.
  Includes bibliographical references and index.
  ISBN 978-1-62031-113-4 (hardcover)
  ISBN 978-1-62496-180-9 (ebook)
  1. Toucans—Juvenile literature. I. Title.
  QL696.P57S38 2015
  598.7'2—dc23
                                    2013044265

Editor: Wendy Dieker
Series Designer: Ellen Huber
Book Designer: Lindaanne Donohoe
Photo Researcher: Kurtis Kinneman

Photo Credits: All photos by Shutterstock except: Alamy, 4; Biosphoto, 8–9, 13; Paolo De Marchi, 20–21; SuperStock, 6–7, 14–15; Visuals Unlimited, 10

Printed in the United States of America at Corporate Graphics, North Mankato, Minnesota.
6-2014
10 9 8 7 6 5 4 3 2 1

Table of Contents

Big Bills

A toucan sits high in a tree.

He lives in the rain forest.

The toucan is hungry.

He looks for food.

He hops from branch
to branch.

He picks cherries.
He reaches them
with his long bill.

He tosses back his head.

Gulp!

Yummy fruit!

Look! A papaya!

He tears off pieces with his sharp bill.

Here is a fig!

He tosses it
to a friend.

They play catch.

fig

Oh no!
A hawk!

16

The toucan flashes his bright bill.

The hawk is scared.

Croak! Croak!

The toucan sounds
like a frog.

He is loud!

The toucan rests
his bill on his back.

Shh! It's time
to sleep.

21

Parts of a Toucan

bill
Toucan bills look heavy, but they are light.

wings
Toucans have short, round wings.

toes
Toucans grip tree branches with their strong toes.

Picture Glossary

fig
A small, sweet fruit with small seeds.

papaya
A yellow or orange sweet fruit that looks like a melon.

hawk
A large bird with a hooked beak that eats other animals.

rain forest
A thick area of trees where a lot of rain falls.

Index

To Learn More

Learning more is as easy as 1, 2, 3.

1) Go to www.factsurfer.com

2) Enter "toucans" into the search box.

3) Click the "Surf" button to see a list of websites.

With factsurfer.com, finding more information is just a click away.